Tyler the Type 1 T-Rex

An Epic Story about a Dinosaur with Diabetes

Tyler the Type 1 T-Rex

Copyright © 2023 by Josh Hall (Gilda Books)

All rights reserved. No part of this book may be used or reproduced in any manner whatsoever without written permission except in the case of brief quotations embodied in critical articles or reviews.

ISBN: 9781991188533
First Edition: May 2023

The information presented is the author's opinion and does not constitute any health or medical advice. The content of this book is for entertainment purposes only and is not intended to diagnose, treat, cure, or prevent any condition or disease.

Contact the author:
Josh Hall - jdj.hall@gmail.com

This book is dedicated to all the Type 1 legends around the world.

Every weekend, Tyler and his two best friends trained for the annual raft race.

They entered the race every year, but no matter how hard they tried, they could never beat the fearsome *Rowdy Rascals*.

But this year might be *different*.
Tyler had grown and grown...

And with a SWISH of his long tail, his team was faster than ever!

But lately, Tyler had been feeling *strange*...

Sometimes he felt *so thirsty* he thought he could drink the entire river.

Sometimes Tyler felt *tired* and *wobbly*, and his tail simply would not swish.

Tyler went to the hospital and visited the doctor.

The doctor explained that his body could not make *insulin* anymore.

Insulin is something everyone needs. It helps move sugar from the blood into the body for energy.

When Tyler's blood glucose went too high, he felt tired, thirsty, and **CRANKY**.

When Tyler took insulin, it helped bring his blood sugar back down.

When Tyler's blood glucose went *too low*, Tyler would feel *weak, shaky* and **SWEATY**.

When this happened, he needed *fast sugar* — like juice or a snack — to bring his blood sugar back up.

It took practice, and sometimes it was tricky.

But soon, Tyler learned more and more about keeping his blood glucose in a healthy range.

When he did, he started to feel totally normal.

In fact...

On the day of the big race, Tyler watched from the shore.

His friends paddled hard, but they were falling behind.

Then suddenly...

...and together the team crossed the line in *first place!*

MORE TYPE 1 ADVENTURES!

AVAILABLE ON AMAZON

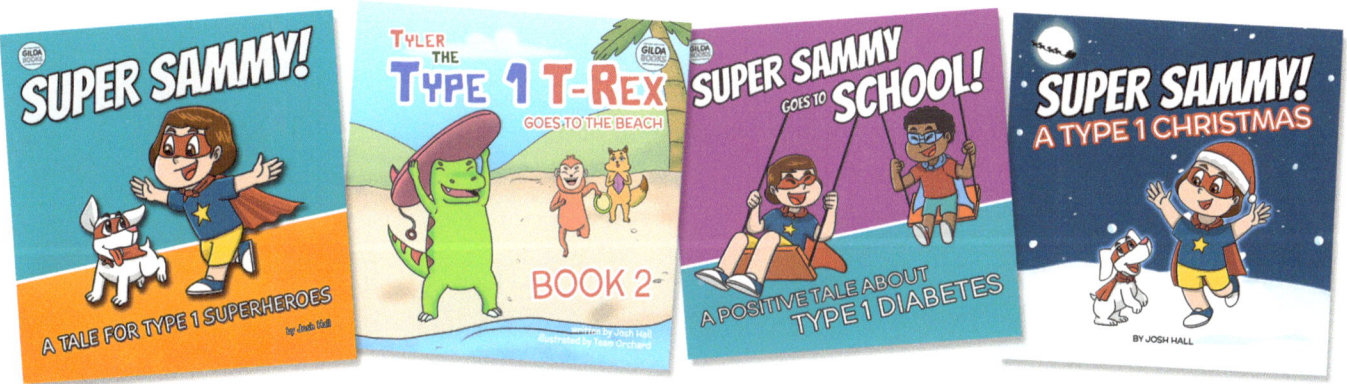

If this story helped your child feel brave,
there are more adventures waiting.

Scan below to see the full Type 1 collection.

If you enjoyed this book, a quick review on Amazon
helps other families find these stories.

DID YOU SPOT ME HIDING IN THIS BOOK??

www.ingramcontent.com/pod-product-compliance
Lightning Source LLC
Chambersburg PA
CBHW041404010526
44107CB00015B/1069